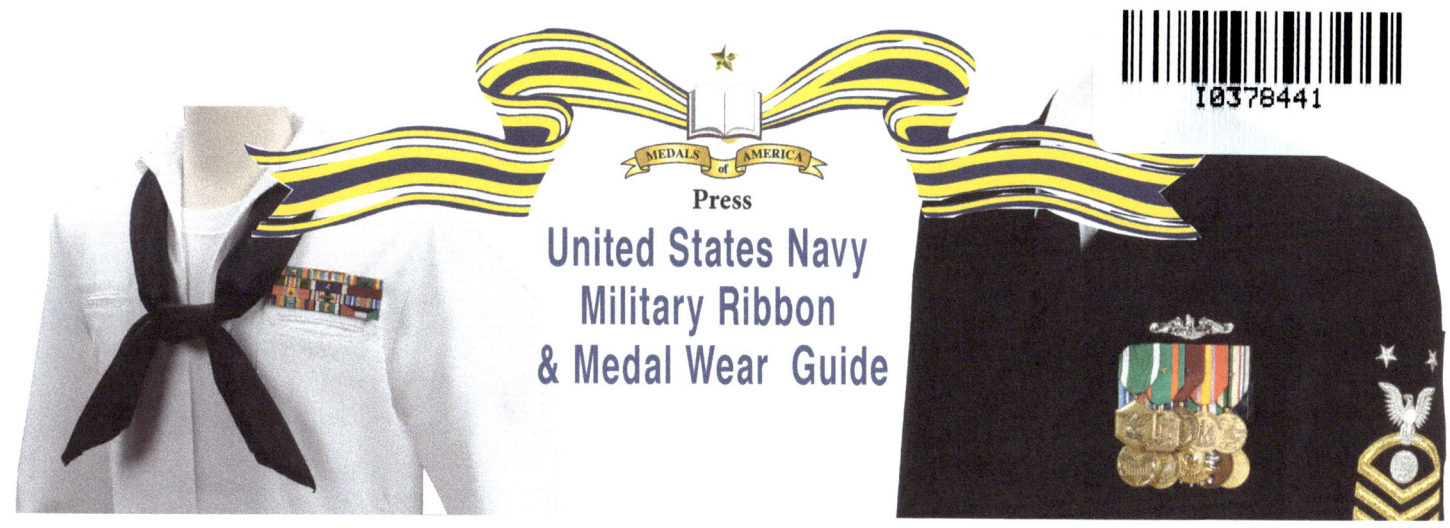

United States Navy Military Ribbon & Medal Wear Guide

We receive just as many questions from veterans as we do active duty and reserve Naval personnel so you will see that the ribbon chart display includes World War II, Korea and Vietnam awards as well as the latest medals such as the Inherent Resolve Campaign Medal.

We have tried to use as many illustrations as possible to make this booklet as clear and user friendly as possible. The new "V", "C" and "R" devices as defined by USN published policy guidance are shown in the ribbon display chest.

Contact us with any suggestions or for any Navy medals, ribbons or insignia at www.usmedals.com

Thank you!

Navy Medals and Ribbons Introduction	2-3
History of Armed Forces Service Ribbons	4-5
Types of Navy Ribbons	6
Navy Ribbons and Devices	7
Navy Multi Service Ribbon Guide	8-9
Placement of Devices and UN Ribbons	10-11
Navy Ribbon and Medal Devices	12-16
Wear of ribbon over right breast pocket	16
Officer, CPO, E1-E6 Ribbon and Medal wear	17-24
Medal chart	Back

Copyright © 2020 by Medals of America Press. All rights reserved. No part of this publication may be reproduced, stored in a retreival system or transmitted by any means, electronic, mechanical or by photocopying without written persmission from the publishers. **ISBN 978-1-884452-26-0**

Published by:
Medals of America Press
114 Southchase Blvd.
Fountain Inn, SC 29644

For additional information on full sized medals, ribbons or skill and qualification badges go to **www.usmedals.com**

Wearing Navy Awards, Order of Precedence and Attachments

(USN photo)

The United States Navy awards system has evolved into a highly structured program often called the "Pyramid of Honor." The system is designed to reward services ranging from heroism on the battlefield to superior performance of non combat duties and even includes the completion of entry level Navy training.

After World War II and Korea the Navy has generally embraced Napoleon's concept of liberally awarding medals and ribbons to enhance morale and esprit de corps. Over the years an expanded and specifically-tailored awards program became generally very popular in the all-volunteer Navy and has played a significant part in improving morale, job performance, recruitment and reenlistments among junior officers and enlisted personnel.

The various ways of wearing decorations and awards by active duty, reserve and veterans are shown on the following pages. These awards paint a wonderful portrait of the Navy's men and women whose dedication to the ideals of freedom represent the rich United States Naval military heritage.

Ribbon Chart Showing the Complete History of U.S. Military Awards

This one of a kind chart on pages 6-7, reads left to right and shows the ribbon for every United States military award since 1861 with many of the variations used. The chart is a colorful walk through our Military awards history.

Navy Order of Precedence Ribbon Chart

On page 9 the current correct order of precedence for Navy ribbons is shown going back to World War II. Authorized attachments for each ribbon are displayed below the ribbon and a reference bar on the right side of the page provides guides to a detailed graphic.

Next is the Navy Order of Precedence Chart for Multi service awards. Veterans who have service in multiple branches of the Armed Forces can determine their military ribbon order of precedence beginning on page 10.

Navy Ribbon Devices *(Appurtenances)* start on page 13 and all Navy ribbon devices are shown as correctly mounted to ribbons and medals. All Navy ribbon devices are shown in alphabetical order starting with the Gold Airplane. For those who desire even more detail charts for proper placement of Navy Ribbon Devices *(Appurtenances)* start on pages 15.

Wearing military ribbons, miniature medals and full size medals on Navy uniforms.

Starting on page 18 are examples along with a brief description of Naval regulations governing current wear.

Variations of a United States Military Medal

Regulation Ribbon Bar

Mini Ribbon*, these are the width of miniature medal ribbon.

Enamel Lapel Pin

Enamel Hat Pin*

Full Size Medal
Used in display cases and mounted for wear by active duty and Reserve Naval personnel

Full Size Anodized Medals (Gold plated) Used in display cases and mounted for wear Washington Naval Ceremonial Units.

Miniature Medals are made in brass or Anodized (Gold plated). Miniature medals are generally only mounted for wear.

Enamel Hat Pins* & Mini Ribbons* are an unofficial item requested by Veterans for wear on unofficial clothing.

Navy Ribbons are mounted three to a row for wear.

US Navy Regulations Medals mounted for wear.

US Navy Regular Brass Miniature Medals mounted for wear.

A History of United States Armed Forces Decorations, Unit Awards & Service Ribbons

Medal of Honor	Medal of Honor Civil War	Medal of Honor Army-1896	Medal of Honor (Original Width)	Marine Corps Brevet Medal	Distinguished Service Cross	Distinguished Service Cross ("French Cut")	Navy Cross	Navy Cross (1st Ribbon)
Air Force Cross	Coast Guard Cross	Certificate of Merit (Obsolete)	Defense Distinguished Service Medal	Army Distinguished Service Medal	Army Disting. Service Medal ("French Cut")	Navy Distinguished Service Medal	Navy Dist. Service Medal (1st Ribbon)	Air Force Distinguished Service Medal
Homeland Security Dist. Service Medal	Transportation Distinguished Service Medal	Coast Guard Distinguished Service Medal	Silver Star	D.O.T. Secty Outstanding Achievement	Defense Superior Service Medal	Transportation Guardian Medal (Coast Guard)	Legion of Merit (Chief Commander)	Legion of Merit (Commander)
Legion of Merit Officer	Legion of Merit (Legionnaire)	Legion of Merit (Neck Ribbon)	Distinguished Flying Cross	Soldier's Medal	Navy and Marine Corps Medal	Airman's Medal	Coast Guard Medal	Coast Guard Medal (not used)
Bronze Star Medal	Purple Heart	Defense Meritorious Service Medal	Meritorious Service Medal	Air Medal	Aerial Achievement Medal	D.O.T. Secy's Meritorious Achvm't Medal	Joint Service Commendation Medal	Army Commendation Medal
Navy & Marine Corps Commendation Medal	Air Force Commendation Medal	Coast Guard Commendation Medal	D.O.T. Secy's Superior Achievement Medal	Joint Service Achievement Medal	Army Achievement Medal	Navy & USMC Achievement Medal	Air Force Achievement Medal	Transportation 9-11 Medal (Coast Guard)
Coast Guard Achievement Medal	USCG Commandant's Letter of Commendation	Navy & Marine Corps Combat Action Ribbon	Air Force Combat Action Medal	Coast Guard Combat Action Ribbon	Wound Ribbon (1917) (Never Issued)	Army Presidential Unit Citation	Navy Presidential Unit Citation	Air Force Presidential Unit Citation
Coast Guard Presidential Unit Citation	Joint Meritorious Unit Award	Army Valorous Unit Award	Air Force Gallant Unit Citation	Navy Unit Commendation	Army Meritorious Unit Commendation	Air Force Meritorious Unit Award	Navy Meritorious Unit Commendation	Air Force Outstanding Unit Award
Air Force Org. Excellence Award	Army Superior Unit Award	D.O.T. Secy's Outstanding Unit Award	Coast Guard Unit Commendation	Coast Guard Meritorious Unit Commendation	Coast Guard Meritorious Team Comndatn	Navy "E" Ribbon	Coast Guard "E" Ribbon	Coast Guard Bicentenniel Unit Commendation
Gold Lifesaving Medal	Silver Lifesaving Medal	Prisoner of War Medal	Air Force Combat Readiness Medal	Army Good Conduct Medal	Reserve Special Commendation Ribbon	Navy Good Conduct Medal	Navy Good Conduct Medal (2nd Ribbon)	Navy Good Conduct Medal (1st Ribbon)
Navy Good Conduct Badge (1869-84)	Marine Corps Good Conduct Medal	Marine Good Conduct Medal (1st Ribbon)	Air Force Good Conduct Medal	Coast Guard Good Conduct Medal	U.S.C.G. Good Conduct Medal (1st Ribbon)	Army Reserve Components Achvm't Medal	Naval Reserve Meritorious Service Medal	Selected Marine Corps Reserve Medal
Fleet Marine Force Reserve Medal- (Obs.)	Air Reserve Forces Meritor's Service Medal	Coast Guard Reserve Good Conduct Medal	Coast Guard Enlisted Person of the Year	Navy Fleet Marine Force Ribbon	Outstanding Airman of the Year Ribbon	Air Force Recognition Ribbon	Civil War Campaign Medal (1861-65)	Civil War Campaign (1st Army Ribbon)
Indian Campaign Medal (1865-91)	Indian Campaign Medal (1st Ribbon)	Dewey Medal (1898)	Sampson Medal (1898)	Spanish Campaign Medal (1898)	Spanish Campaign Medal (1st Army Ribbon)	Spanish Campaign Medal (1st Navy Ribbon)	Cardenas Medal of Honor (1898)	Specially Meritorious Medal (1898)
West Indies Campaign Medal (1898)	West Indies Campaign (1st Ribbon)	Spanish War Service Medal (1898)	Cuban Occupation Medal (1898-1902)	Puerto Rican Occupation Medal (1898)	Philippine Campaign Medal (1899 - 1913)	Philippine Campaign (1st Navy Ribbon)	Philippine Congressional Medal (1899-1902)	China Campaign Medal (1900-01)

A History of United States Armed Forces Decorations, Unit Awards & Service Ribbons

China Relief Expedition (1st Navy Ribbon)	Cuban Pacification Medal (1906-09)	Peary Polar Expedit'n Medal (1908-09)	Mexican Service Medal (1911-17)	1st Nicaraguan Campaign Medal (1912)	Haitian Campaign Medal (1915)	Dominican Campaign Medal (1916)	Mexican Border Service Medal (1916-17)	World War I Victory Medal (1917 - 18)
Texas Cavalry Congressional Medal (1918)	Occupation of Germany (1918-23)	N.C.-4 Medal (1919)	Haitian Campaign Medal (1919-20)	2nd Nicaraguan Camp'n Medal (1926-33)	Yangtze Service Medal (1926-32)	1st Byrd Antarctic Expedit'n (1928-30)	Navy Expeditionary Medal	Marine Corps Expeditionary Medal
2nd Byrd Antarctic Expedit'n (1933-35)	China Service Medal (1937, 1945)	Amer. Defense Service Medal (1939-41)	Women's Army Corps Service Medal	American Campaign Medal (1941-46)	Asiatic-Pacific Camp'n Medal (1941-46)	Europe-African-Mid East Campaign	World War II Victory Medal (1941 - 46)	U.S. Antarctic Expedit'n Medal (1939-41)
World War II Occupat'n Medal (1945-57)	Medal for Humane Action (1948-49)	Nat'l Defense Service Medal (1950, 61, 90, 01)	Korean Service Medal (1950-54)	Antarctica Service Medal	Coast Guard Arctic Service Medal	Armed Forces Expeditionary Medal	Vietnam Service Medal (1965-73)	Southwest Asia Service Medal (1991-95)
Kosovo Campaign Medal (1999-)	Afghanistan Campaign Medal (2001-)	Iraq Campaign Medal (2003 - 11)	Inherent Resolve Campaign Medal	War on Terrorism Expeditionary Medal (2001-)	War on Terrorism Service Medal (2001-)	Korea Defense Service Medal (1954-)	Armed Forces Service Medal	Humanitarian Service Medal
Outstanding Volunteer Service Medal	Navy Sea Service Deployment Ribbon	Navy Arctic Service Ribbon	Naval Reserve Sea Service Ribbon	Navy & Marine Corps Overseas Service Ribbon	Navy Recruiting Service Ribbon	Navy Recruit Training Service Ribbon	Navy Ceremonial Guard Ribbon	Navy Recruit Honor Graduate Ribbon
Marine Corps Recruiting Ribbon	Marine Corps Drill Instructor Ribbon	Marine Security Guard Ribbon	Marine Corps Combat Instructor Ribbon	Air Force Air & Space Campaign Medal	USAF Nuclear Deterrence Opns Medal	Air Force Overseas Ribbon (Short Tour)	Air Force Overseas Ribbon (Long Tour)	Air Force Expeditionary Service Ribbon
Air Force Longevity Service Award Ribbon	Air Force Special Duty Ribbon	Air Force Military Training Instructor Rib'n	Air Force Recruiter Ribbon	Transportation 9-11 Ribbon (Coast Guard)	Coast Guard Special Oper'ns Service Ribbon	Coast Guard Sea Service Ribbon	Coast Guard Restricted Duty Ribbon	Coast Guard Overseas Service Ribbon
Coast Guard Basic Training Honor Graduate Ribbon	Coast Guard Recruiting Service Ribbon	Army Sea Duty Ribbon	Armed Forces Reserve Medal	Army NCO Prof. Development Ribbon	Army Service Ribbon	Army Overseas Service Ribbon	Army Reserve Comp. Overseas Training Ribbon	Naval Reserve Medal (Obsolete)
Marine Corps Reserve Ribbon (Obsolete)	Air Force NCO Prof. Military Education Grad.	Air Force Basic Military Training Honor Graduate	Air Force Small Arms Expert Marksman	Air Force Training Ribbon	Philippine Presidential Unit Citation	Korean Presidential Unit Citation	Vietnam Presidential Unit Citation	Vietnam Gallantry Cross Unit Citation
Vietnam Civil Actions Unit Citation	Philippine Defense Ribbon	Philippine Liberation Ribbon (1944 - 45)	Philippine Independence Ribbon (1946)	United Nations Korean Service Medal	UN Palestine Mission (UNTSO)	UN India/Pakistan Mission (UNMOGIP)	UN New Guinea Mission (UNTEA)	UN Iraq/Kuwait Mission (UNIKOM)
UN Western Sahara Mission (MINURSO)	UN Cambodia Mission 1 (UNAMIC)	UN Yugoslavia Mission (UNPROFOR)	UN Cambodia Mission 2 (UNTAC)	UN Somalia Mission (UNOSOM)	UN Haiti Mission (UNMIH)	UN Special Service Medal (UNSSM)	NATO Medal for Bosnia	NATO Medal for Kosovo
NATO Medal for Operation Eagle Assist	NATO Medal for Operation Active Endeavor	NATO Medal for Balkan Operations	NATO Medal for Afghanistan, Sudan, Iraq	Multinational Force & Observers Medal	Inter-American Defense Board Medal	Republic of Vietnam Campaign Medal	Kuwait Liberation Medal (Saudi Arabia)	Kuwait Liberation Medal (Kuwait)
Republic of Korea War Service Medal	Navy Distinguished Marksman Badge	Navy Distinguished Pistol Shot Badge	Navy Dist. Marksman & Pistol Shot	Navy Rifle Marksmanship Ribbon	Navy Pistol Marksmanship Ribbon	Coast Guard Dist. Marksman & Pistol Shot	Coast Guard Rifle Marksmanship Ribbon	Coast Guard Pistol Marksmanship Ribbon

Types of Medals, Ribbons and Attachments

Decoration - An award conferred on an individual for a specific act of gallantry or for meritorious service.

There are two general categories of "medals" awarded by the United States to its military personnel, namely, decorations and service medals.

The terms "decoration" and "medal" are used almost interchangeably today *(as they are in this book)*, but there are recognizable distinctions between them. Decorations, are awarded for acts of gallantry and meritorious service and usually have distinctive *(and often unique)* shapes such as crosses or stars.

Medal-An individual award presented for performance of certain duties or to those who have participated in designated wars, campaigns, expeditions, etc., or who have fulfilled specified service requirements.

Medals are awarded for good conduct, participation in a particular campaign or expedition, or a noncombatant service and normally come in a round shape. Campaign or service medals are issued to individuals who participate in particular campaigns or periods of service for which a medal is authorized. The fact that some very prestigious awards have the word "medal" in their titles *(e.g.: Medal of Honor)*, can cause some confusion.

Unit Awards & Ribbon Only

Unit Award - *An award made to an operating unit for outstanding performance. See the chart to your right.*

Ribbon Only Award - *An award made to an individual for completion of certain training or specific assignment for which there is no medal. See the chart to your right.*

Example - *This example shows three decoration(one from the Army), and other awards you can identify from the chart to your right.*

Attachments and Devices

Attachment - *Any device such as a star, clasp, or other appurtenance worn on a suspension ribbon of a medal or on the ribbon bar (also called device). See pages 14 and 15 for all.*

Bronze and Silver Service Stars

A bronze star is worn on suspension ribbons of large and miniature medals and ribbon bars to indicate a second or subsequent award or to indicate major engagements in which an individual participated. Silver Stars - A silver star is worn on suspension ribbons of large and miniature medals and ribbon bars in lieu of five bronze stars.

Letter "V"

A bronze letter "V" is worn on specific combat decorations if the award is approved for valor (heroism). Only one "V" is worn and different Vs are used to indicate additional awards.

Navy Occupation Service Medal Clasp

The bronze Navy of Occupation Medal clasp marked "ASIA" and or "Europe" is worn on suspension ribbons of large and miniature NavyOccupation Medals to denote service in those areas.

Gold and Silver Stars

A Gold starr denotes a second or subsequent award of a personal naval decoration. A silver Silver star is worn in lieu of five bronze Gold Stars

Hour Glass

A bronze hour glass device denotes ten years service on the Armed Forces Reserve Medal. Upon the completion of the ten year period, reservists are awarded the Armed Forces Reserve Medal with a bronze hourglass device. Silver and gold hourglass devices are awarded at the end of twenty and thirty years of reserve service, respectively.

Letter "M"

A bronze letter "M" on the Armed Forces Reserve Medal denotes reservists mobilized and called to active duty.

Oak Leaf Cluster

A bronze Oak Leaf Cluster denotes a second or subsequent award of a personal Dept. of Defense decoration. A silver Oak Leaf Cluster is worn in lieu of five bronze Oak Leaf Clusters.

Bronze Numerals

Denotes total number of awards of the Air Medal and other awards.

Bronze Eagle, Golbe and Anchor *Denotes Service with marine Units.*

New C and R Devices

The C device indicates the award was issued in a comabat zone while the R indicateds the award was presented for action remote from the combat zone.

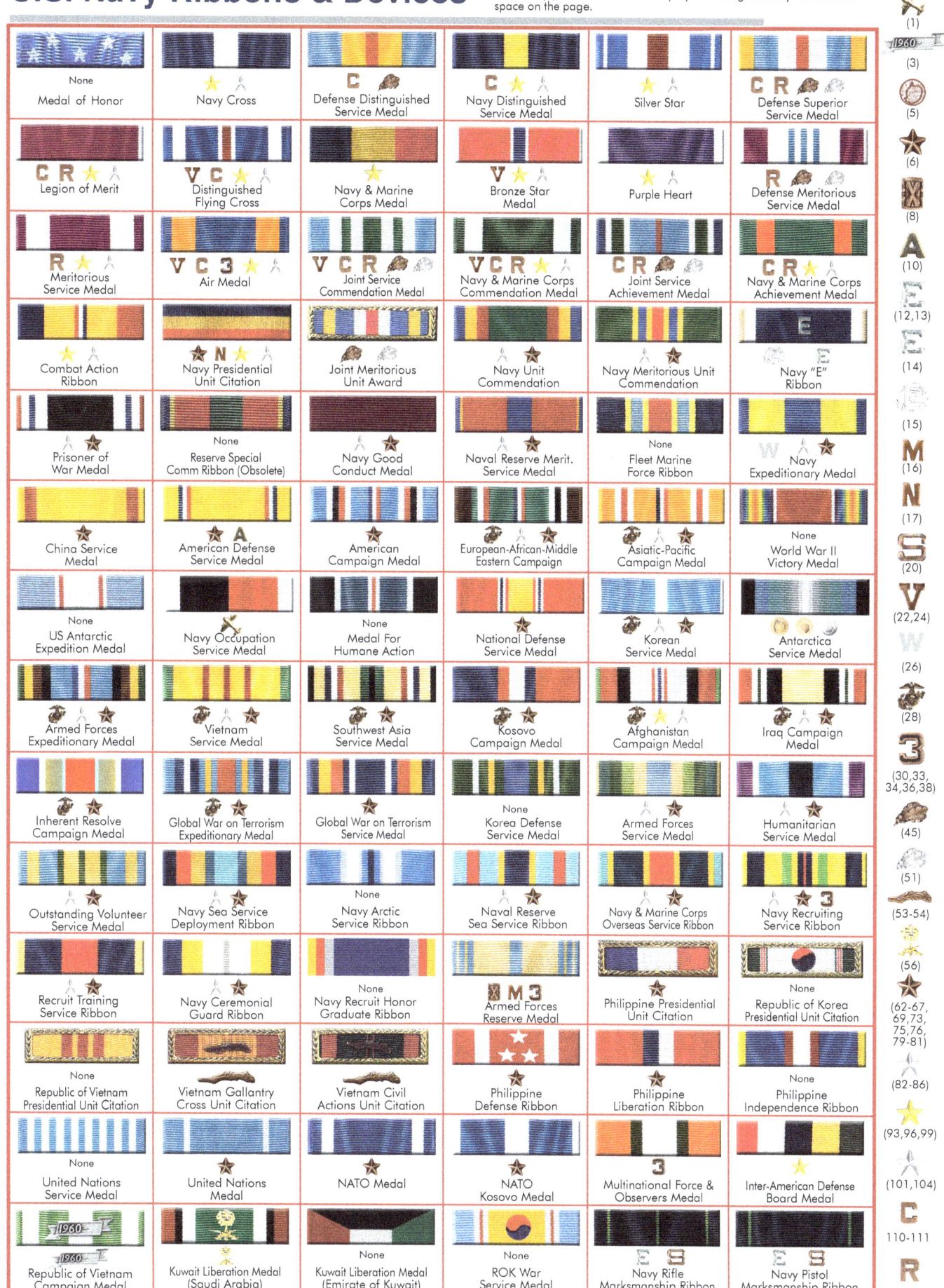

United States Navy Multi Service Decorations, Unit Awards & Service Ribbons Page 1

When Sailors are entitled to similar awards from two or more services; for example, good conduct awards, the Navy award will take precedence. After the navy award, similar awards of other services will be worn in the following precedence: Marines, Army, Air Force, and Coast Guard.

Shown below are examples of Multi service awards and a chart laying out the correct order of wear for naval personnel who have been awarded decorations, unit awards or service medals while assigned or while serving in other branches of the Armed Forces.

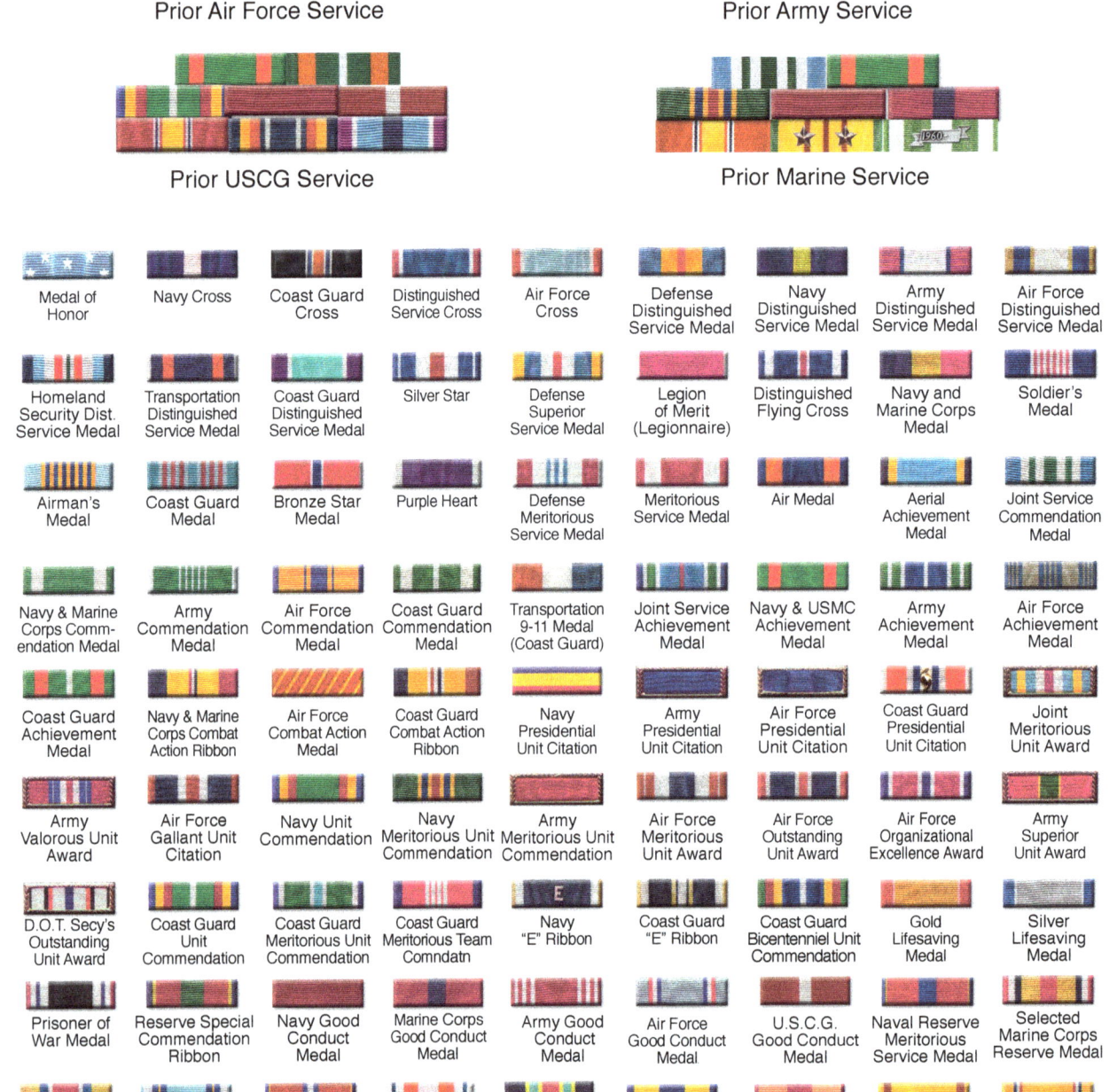

United States Navy Multi Service Decorations, Unit Awards & Service Ribbons Page 2

Women's Army Corps Service Medal	American Campaign Medal (1941-46)	Europe-African-Mid East Cam-p'gn	Asiatic-Pacific Camp'n Medal (1941-46)	World War II Victory Medal (1941 - 46)	U.S. Antarctic Expedit'n Medal (1939-41)	World War II Occupat'n Medal (1945-57)	Medal for Humane Action (1948-49)	Nat'l Defense Service Medal (1950, 61, 90, 01)
Korean Service Medal (1950-54)	Antarctica Service Medal	Coast Guard Arctic Service Medal	Armed Forces Expeditionary Medal	Vietnam Service Medal (1965-73)	Southwest Asia Service Medal (1991-95)	Kosovo Campaign Medal (1999-)	Afghanistan Campaign Medal (2001 -)	Iraq Campaign Medal (2003 - 11)
Inherent Resolve Campaign Medal	War on Terrorism Expeditionary Medal (2001-)	War on Terrorism Service Medal (2001-)	Korea Defense Service Medal (1954-)	Armed Forces Service Medal	Humanitarian Service Medal	Outstanding Volunteer Service Medal	Navy Sea Service Deployment Ribbon	Navy Arctic Service Ribbon
Naval Reserve Sea Service Ribbon	Navy & Marine Corps Overseas Service Ribbon	Navy Recruiting Service Ribbon	Marine Corps Recruiting Ribbon	Marine Corps Drill Instructor Ribbon	Marine Security Guard Ribbon	Marine Corps Combat Instructor Ribbon	Navy Recruit Training Service Ribbon	Navy Ceremonial Guard Ribbon
Navy Recruit Honor Graduate Ribbon	Transportation 9-11 Ribbon (Coast Guard)	Coast Guard Special Oper'ns Service Ribbon	Coast Guard Sea Service Ribbon	Coast Guard Restricted Duty Ribbon	Coast Guard Overseas Service Ribbon	CG Basic Tng Honor Graduate Ribbon	Coast Guard Recruiting Service Ribbon	Air Force Air & Space Campaign Medal
USAF Nuclear Deterrence Opns Medal	Air Force Overseas Ribbon (Short Tour)	Air Force Overseas Ribbon (Long Tour)	Air Force Expeditionary Service Ribbon	Air Force Longevity Service Award Ribbon	Air Force Special Duty Ribbon	Air Force Military Training Instructor Rib'n	Air Force Recruiter Ribbon	Army Sea Duty Ribbon
Armed Forces Reserve Medal	Naval Reserve Medal (Obsolete)	Marine Corps Reserve Ribbon (Obsolete)	Army NCO Prof. Development Ribbon	Army Service Ribbon	Army Overseas Service Ribbon	Army Reserve Comp. Overseas Training Ribbon	Air Force NCO Prof. Military Education Grad.	Air Force Basic Military Training Honor Graduate
Air Force Small Arms Expert Marksman	Air Force Training Ribbon	Philippine Presidential Unit Citation	Korean Presidential Unit Citation	Vietnam Presidential Unit Citation	Vietnam Gallantry Cross Unit Citation	Vietnam Civil Actions Unit Citation	Philippine Defense Ribbon	Philippine Liberation Ribbon (1944 - 45)
Philippine Independence Ribbon (1946)	United Nations Korean Service Medal	UN Palestine Mission (UNTSO)	UN India/Pakistan Mission (UNMOGIP)	UN New Guinea Mission (UNTEA)	UN Iraq/Kuwait Mission (UNIKOM)	UN Western Sahara Mission (MINURSO)	UN Cambodia Mission 1 (UNAMIC)	UN Yugoslavia Mission (UNPROFOR)
UN Cambodia Mission 2 (UNTAC)	UN Somalia Mission (UNOSOM)	UN Haiti Mission (UNMIH)	UN Special Service Medal (UNSSM)	NATO Medal for Bosnia	NATO Medal for Kosovo	NATO Medal for Operation Eagle Assist	NATO Medal for Operation Active Endeavor	NATO Medal for Balkan Operations
NATO Medal for Afghanistan, Sudan, Iraq	Multinational Force & Observers Medal	Inter-American Defense Board Medal	Republic of Vietnam Campaign Medal	Kuwait Liberation Medal (Saudi Arabia)	Kuwait Liberation Medal (Kuwait)	Republic of Korea War Service Medal	Navy Distinguished Marksman Badge	Navy Distinguished Pistol Badge
Navy Dist. Marksman & Pistol Shot	Navy Rifle Marksmanship Ribbon	Navy Pistol Marksmanship Ribbon	Coast Guard Dist. Marksman & Pistol Shot	Coast Guard Rifle Marksmanship Ribbon	Coast Guard Pistol Marksmanship Ribbon			

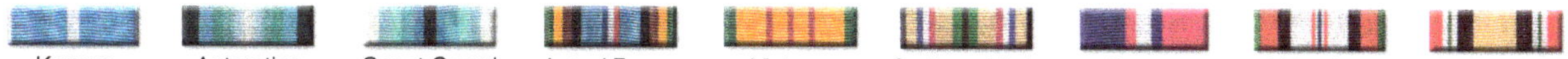

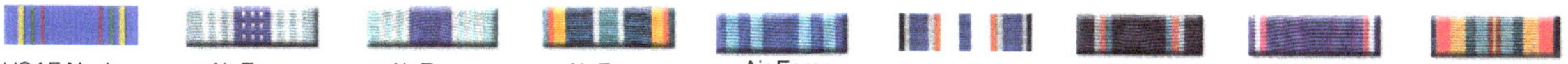

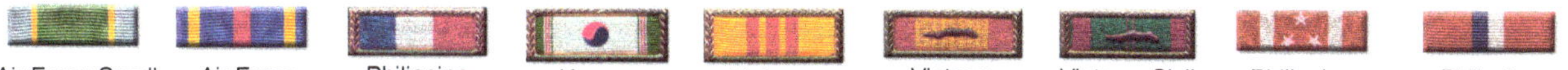

Multi Service Ribbons Not Authorized by the United States Navy

(Basically the Navy does not authorize ribbons for which it does not have an equivalent ribbon.)

Air Force Combat Readiness Medal

USCG Comman-dant's Letter of Commendation

Outstanding Airman of the Year Ribbon

Air Force Recognition Ribbon

Placement of Recent Campaign Stars on Ribbons

Over the past decade there has been confusion on the number of campaign stars individual sailors have earned for service in Iraq and Afghanistan. Shown below is a summary of the campaigns as of 2019 for both the Iraq and Afghanistan campaign medals. To date there have been six campaign stars authorized in Afghanistan and seven campaign stars authorized for service in Iraq.

Bronze and silver campaign stars designate the number of campaign phases in which a sailor has served. One days service during any phase earns a bronze campaign star to be worn on the service medal. Service in five different phases of a campaigns is indicated by a silver campaign star. The campaign stars indicate how many phases in which a sailor has participated and do not represent additional awards of the respective campaign medal. One campaign star is worn on a suspension ribbon of the medal or on the ribbon bar for one or more days of service in each designated campaign phase.

The Afghanistan Campaign Medal and the Iraq Campaign Medal will always be awarded with at least one bronze campaign star. The policy is the same for the Southwest Asia Service Medal, the Vietnam Service Medal and the Korean Service Medal. If a sailor's service extends at least one day into a subsequent campaign phase then an additional bronze campaign star is awarded.

See the examples on the next page which shows the correct placements of campaign stars for participating from one to seven phases in Iraq.

Iraq	Campaign	Medal
Phase	From	To
Phase 1: Liberation of Iraq	March 19, 2003	May 1, 2003
Phase 2: Transition of Iraq	May 2, 2003	June 28, 2004
Phase 3: Iraqi Governance	June 29, 2004	December 15, 2005
Phase 4: National Resolution	December 16, 2005	January 9, 2007
Phase 5: Iraqi Surge	January 10, 2007	December 31, 2008
Phase 6: Iraqi Sovereignty	January 1, 2009	August 31, 2010
Phase 7: New Dawn	September 1, 2010	December 31, 2011

Afghanistan	Campaign	Medal
Phase Name	From	To
Phase 1: Liberation of Afghanistan	September 11, 2001	November 30, 2001
Phase 2: Consolidation I	December 1, 2001	September 30, 2006
Phase 3: Consolidation II	October 1, 2006	November 30, 2009
Phase 4: Consolidation III	December 1, 2009	June 30, 2011
Phase 5: Transition I	July 1, 2011	December 31, 2014
Phase 6: Transition II	January 1, 2015	Present

United Nations Ribbons for Wear on the U.S. Navy Uniform

Only one United Nations Ribbon maybe worn. A second or additional award of a United Nations Service Medal is indicated by a 3/16s Bronze Star.

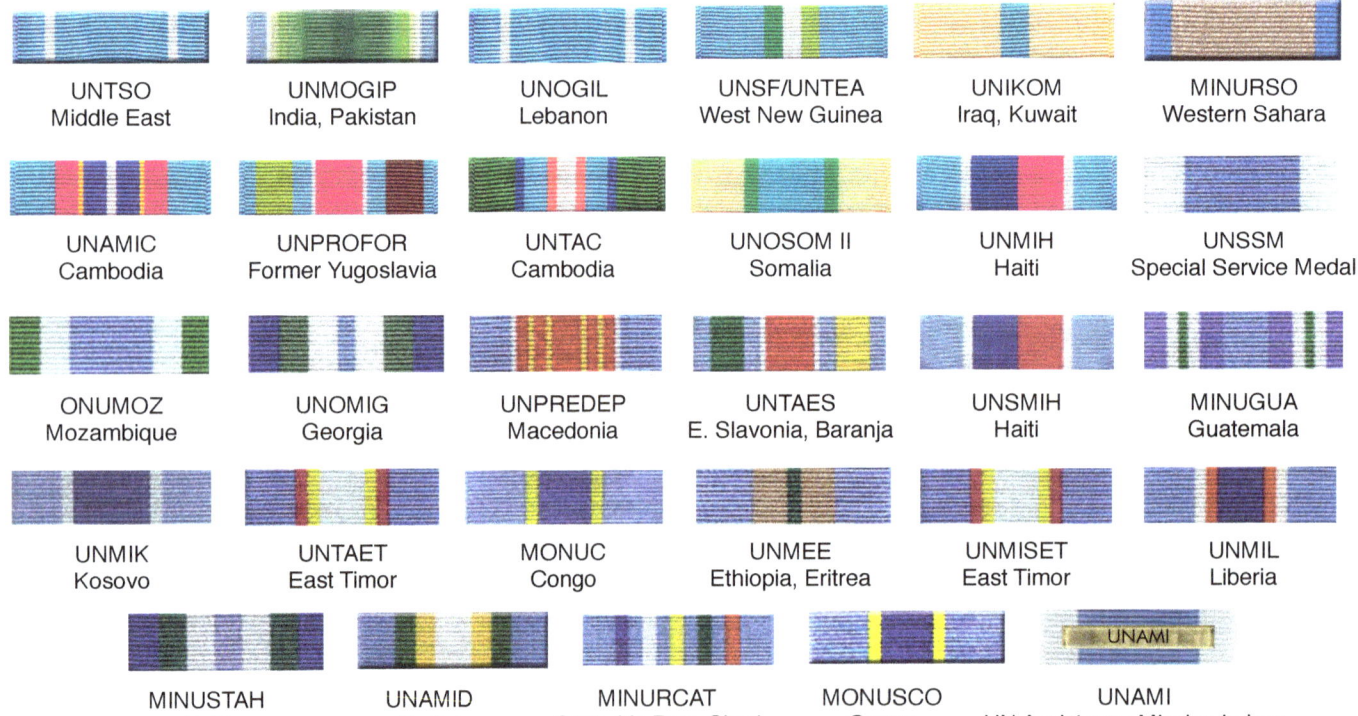

UNTSO - Middle East
UNMOGIP - India, Pakistan
UNOGIL - Lebanon
UNSF/UNTEA - West New Guinea
UNIKOM - Iraq, Kuwait
MINURSO - Western Sahara

UNAMIC - Cambodia
UNPROFOR - Former Yugoslavia
UNTAC - Cambodia
UNOSOM II - Somalia
UNMIH - Haiti
UNSSM - Special Service Medal

ONUMOZ - Mozambique
UNOMIG - Georgia
UNPREDEP - Macedonia
UNTAES - E. Slavonia, Baranja
UNSMIH - Haiti
MINUGUA - Guatemala

UNMIK - Kosovo
UNTAET - East Timor
MONUC - Congo
UNMEE - Ethiopia, Eritrea
UNMISET - East Timor
UNMIL - Liberia

MINUSTAH - Haiti
UNAMID - Darfur
MINURCAT - Cent. Afr. Rep, Chad
MONUSCO - Congo
UNAMI - UN Assistance Mission in Iraq

Placement of Devices on Ribbons

No. of Awards	3/16 Bronze and Silver Campaign Stars	Letter V*	Air Medal Individual	Air Medal Strike Flight
1				1
2				2
3				3
4				4
5				5
6				6
7				7
8				
9				
10				

Air Medal (1980-1989, 2006-2017)
 Bronze Block Numerals
Gold Numerals

Air Medal (1989-2006)

Armed Forces Reserve Medal

After 10 years of reserve service | With 1 mobilization | With 2 mobilizations | After 10 years of reserve service and 3 mobilizations

Legend:

	= Bronze Letter "M"		= 5/16" dia. Gold Star		= Bronze Oak Leaf Cluster
	= Hourglass		= 5/16" dia. Silver Star		= 3/16" dia. Bronze Star
	= Letter "V"		= Bronze Block Numerals		= 3/16" dia. Silver Star

U.S. Navy Ribbon Devices

1. Airplane, C-54, Gold

Services: All
Worn on: World War II Occupation Medals
Denotes: Service during Berlin Airlift (1948-49)

2. Bar, Date, Silver

Services: All
Worn on: Republic of Vietnam Campaign Medal
Denotes: Worn upon initial issue; has no significance

3. Letter "C", Serif, Bronze

Services: All
Worn on: Personal Decorations
Denotes: Award earned in a combat setting.

4a. Disk, Bronze, Gold, Silver

Worn on: Antarctica Service Medal
Denotes: Wintered over 1, 2 or 3 times on the Antarctic continent

7. Globe, Gold

Services: Navy
Worn on: Navy Presidential Unit Citation
Denotes: Service with USS Triton during 1st submerged cruise around the world

5a. Hourglass, Bronze

Services: All
Worn on: Armed Forces Reserve Medal
Denotes: 10 Years of service in the Reserve Forces

5b. Hourglass, Silver

Services: All
Worn on: Armed Forces Reserve Medal
Denotes: 20 Years of service in the Reserve Forces

5c. Hourglass, Gold

Services: All
Worn on: Armed Forces Reserve Medal
Denotes: 30 Years of service in the Reserve Forces

6. Letter "A", Block, Bronze

Services: Navy, Marine Corps, Coast Guard
Worn on: American Defense Service Medal
Denotes: Atlantic Fleet service prior to World War II

7. Letter "E", Block, Silver

Services: Navy, Marine Corps.
Worn on: Navy "E" Ribbon
Denotes: Initial and subsequent awards (3 maximum)

12. Letter "E", Serif, Bronze

Services: Navy, Coast Guard
Worn on: Marksmanship Ribbons
Denotes: First "Expert" qualification **(Obsolete)**

13. Letter "E", Serif, Silver
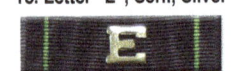
Services: Navy, Coast Guard
Worn on: Marksmanship Ribbons
Denotes: "Expert" weapons qualification

8. Letter "E", Wreathed, Silver

Services: Navy, Marine Corps.
Worn on: Navy "E" Ribbon
Denotes: Fourth (Final) award

9. Letter "M", Block, Bronze

Services: All
Worn on: Armed Forces Reserve Medal
Denotes: Mobilization for active military service

17. Letter "N", Block, Gold

Services: Navy
Worn on: Navy Presidential Unit Citation
Denotes: Service aboard USS Nautilus during 1st cruise under the Arctic ice cap

22. Letter "V", Serif, Bronze

Services: All (Except Marine Corps)
Worn on: Personal decorations
Denotes: Valorous actions in combat

10. Letter "V", Serif, Bronze

Services: All
Worn on: Joint Service Commendation Medal
Denotes: Valorous actions in combat

12. Letter "W", Block, Silver
Services: Navy, Marine Corps.
Worn on: Expeditionary Medals
Denotes: Participation in the defense of Wake Island (Dec, 1941)

27. Maltese Cross, Bronze
Services: Navy
Worn on: World War I Victory Medal
Denotes: Service by Navy personnel with the AEF

28. Marine Device, Bronze

Services: Navy
Worn on: Campaign medals since World War II
Denotes: Service by Naval combat personnel with Marine Corps units

13. Numeral, Block, Bronze

Services: Navy, Marine Corps.
Worn on: Air Medal
Denotes: Total number of Strike/Flight awards

14. Numeral, Block, Bronze

Services: All (Except Coast Guard)
Worn on: Humanitarian Service Medal
Denotes: Number of additional awards *(Obsolete)*

15. Numeral, Block, Bronze

Services: All
Worn on: Armed Forces Reserve Medal
Denotes: Number of times mobilized for active duty

34. Numeral, Block, Bronze

Services: Navy
Worn on: Navy Recruiting Service Ribbon
Denotes: Total number of "Gold Wreath" awards

16. Numeral, Block, Bronze

Services: All
Worn on: Multinational Force & Observers Medal
Denotes: Total number of awards

17. Numeral, Block, Gold

Services: Navy, Marine Corps
Worn on: Air Medal
Denotes: Total number of individual awards

40. Numeral, Scroll, Bronze

Services: Navy
Worn on: World War II Campaign Medals
Denotes: Number of battle clasps earned **(Obsolete)**

45. Oak Leaf Cluster, Bronze

Services: All
Worn on: Joint Service Decorations and Joint Meritorious Unit Award
Denotes: One (1) additional award

21. Palm, Bronze

Services: All (Except Army)
Worn on: Vietnam Gallantry Cross Unit Citation
Denotes: No significance, worn upon initial issue

54. Palm, Bronze

Services: All
Worn on: Vietnam Civil Actions Unit Citation
Denotes: No significance, worn upon initial issue

23. Palm & Swords Device, Gold  **Services:** All **Worn on:** Kuwait Liberation Medal (Saudi Arabia) **Denotes:** No significance, worn upon initial issue	**24. Star 3/16" dia., Blue**  **Services:** Navy, Marine Corps **Worn on:** Navy Presidential Unit Citation **Denotes:** Initial and subsequent awards *(Obsolete)*	**25. Star 3/16" dia., Bronze**  **Services:** All **Worn on:** Campaign awards since World War II **Denotes:** Battle participation	**26. Star 3/16" dia., Bronze**  **Services:** All **Worn on:** Expeditionary Medals **Denotes:** Additional service *(one star per designated expedition)*	**27. Star 3/16" dia., Bronze**  **Services:** All **Worn on:** Prisoner of War and Humanitarian Service Medals **Denotes:** One (1) additional award
28. Star 3/16" dia., Bronze  **Services:** Navy, Marine Corps. **Worn on:** Unit Awards **Denotes:** One (1) star per each additional award	**67. Star 3/16" dia., Bronze**  **Services:** All **Worn on:** Service Awards **Denotes:** One (1) star per each additional award	**68. Star 3/16" dia., Bronze**  **Services:** Navy **Worn on:** Letter of Commendation Ribbon with Pendant **Denotes:** One additional award *(Obsolete)*	**69. Star 3/16" dia., Bronze**  **Services:** Navy and Marine Corps. **Worn on:** Air Medal **Denotes:** First individual award *(Obsolete)*	**72. Star 3/16" dia., Bronze**  **Services:** All **Worn on:** World War I Victory Medal **Denotes:** One (1) star for each campaign clasp earned
73. Star 3/16" dia., Bronze  **Services:** Navy, Marine Corps, Coast Guard **Worn on:** China Service Medal (1937-39) **Denotes:** Additional award for service during (1945-57)	**75. Star 3/16" dia., Bronze**  **Services:** All **Worn on:** American Defense Service Medal **Denotes:** Overseas service prior to World War II	**76. Star 3/16" dia., Bronze**  **Services:** All **Worn on:** National Defense Service Medal **Denotes:** Additional awards (one star per designated period)	**79. Star 3/16" dia., Bronze**  **Services:** All **Worn on:** Philippine Defense and Liberation Ribbons **Denotes:** Additional battle honors	**80. Star 3/16" dia., Bronze**  **Services:** All (Except Army) **Worn on:** Philippine Presidential Unit Citation **Denotes:** Additional award
81. Star 3/16" dia., Bronze  **Services:** All **Worn on:** United Nations and NATO mission medals **Denotes:** One (1) star for each additional mission	**82. Star 3/16" dia., Silver**  **Services:** All **Worn on:** Campaign awards since World War II **Denotes:** Battle participation in five (5) major engagements	**83. Star 3/16" dia., Silver**  **Services:** All **Worn on:** Expeditionary Medals **Denotes:** Five (5) additional expeditions	**84. Star 3/16" dia., Silver**  **Services:** All **Worn on:** Prisoner of War and Humanitarian Service Medals **Denotes:** Five (5) additional awards	**85. Star 3/16" dia., Silver**  **Services:** Navy, Marine Corps **Worn on:** Unit awards **Denotes:** Five (5) additional awards
86. Star 3/16" dia., Silver  **Services:** All **Worn on:** Service Awards **Denotes:** Five (5) additional Awards	**87. Star 3/16" dia., Silver**  **Services:** Navy **Worn on:** World War I Victory Medal **Denotes:** Receipt of Letter of Commendation	**91. Star 5/16" dia., Bronze**  **Services:** Navy, Marine Corps. **Worn on:** Navy, USMC Expeditionary Medals **Denotes:** One (1) additional award *(Obsolete)*	**92. Star 5/16" dia., Bronze**  **Services:** Navy, Marine Corps. **Worn on:** Haitian Campaign Medal (1915) **Denotes:** Subsequent award of the "1919-1920" Clasp	**93. Star 5/16" dia., Gold**  **Services:** Navy, Marine Corps, Coast Guard **Worn on:** Personal Decorations **Denotes:** One (1) additional award
96. Star 5/16" dia., Gold  **Services:** Navy, Marine Corps **Worn on:** Combat Action Ribbon **Denotes:** One (1) additional award	**48. Star 5/16" dia., Gold**  **Services:** All **Worn on:** Inter-American Defense Board Medal **Denotes:** One (1) additional award	**101. Star 5/16" dia., Silver**  **Services:** Navy, Marine Corps, Coast Guard **Worn on:** Personal Decorations **Denotes:** Five (5) additional awards	**104. Star 5/16" dia., Silver**  **Services:** Navy **Worn on:** World War II Campaign Medals **Denotes:** Five (5) major campaigns *(Obsolete)*	**51. Letter "R", serif, Bronze**  **Services:** All **Worn on:** Personal Decorations **Denotes:** Recognizes remote combat action

Examples of Navy Ribbons and Devices

Placement of the Letter "V" (Valor) and Gold & Silver Stars

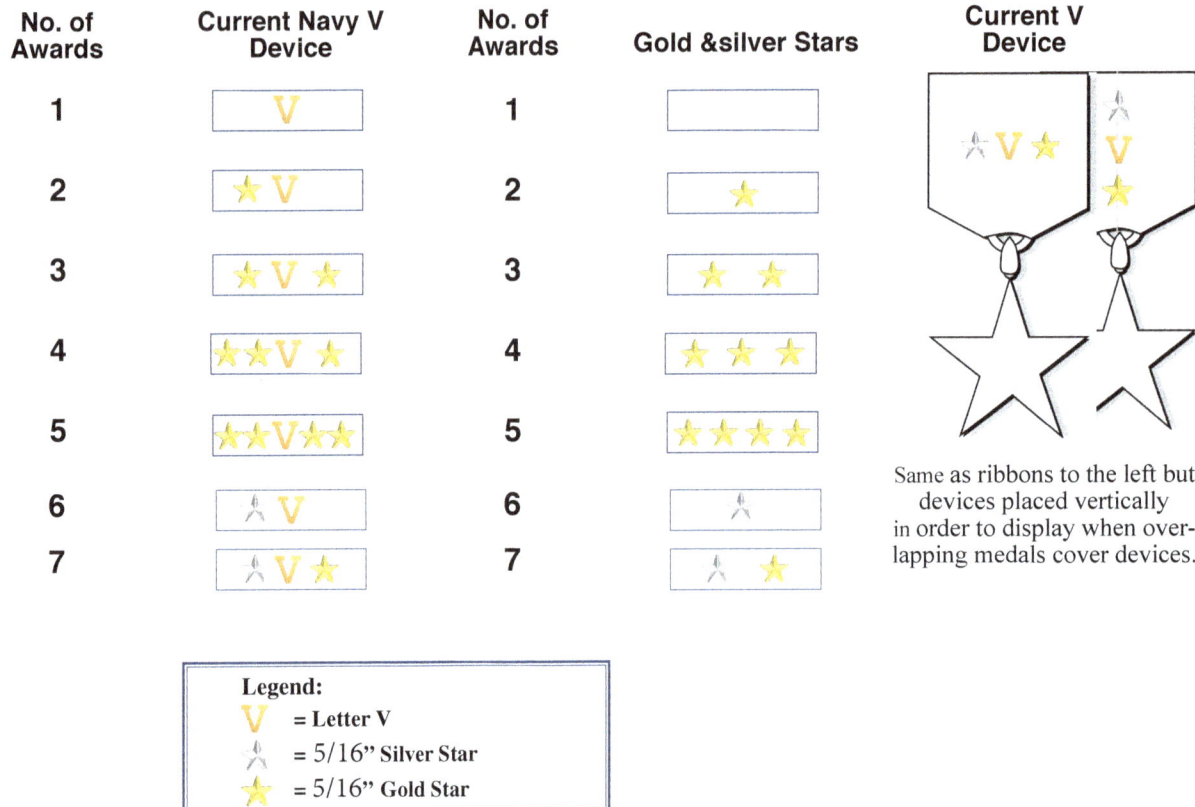

Placement of Devices on the Armed Forces Reserve Medal

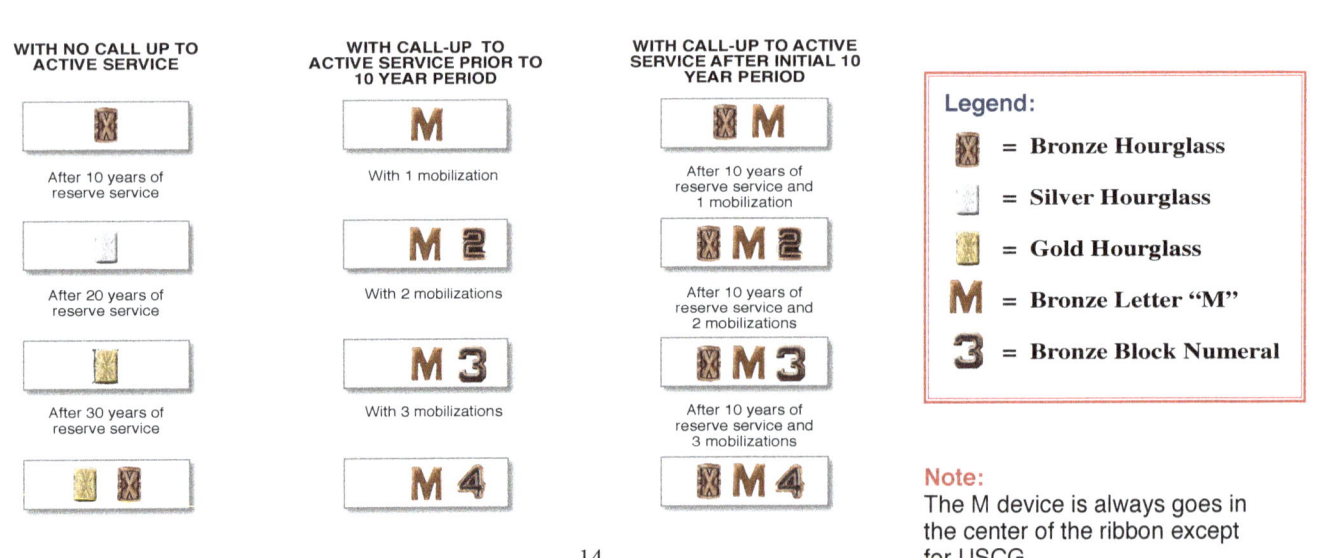

Placement of Bronze and Silver Campaign Stars

No. of Campaigns	Navy	No. of Campaigns	Navy
1	★	6	☆ ★
2	★ ★	7	★ ☆ ★
3	★ ★ ★	8	★ ★ ☆ ★
4	★ ★ ★ ★	9	★ ★ ★ ★ ★
5	☆	10	☆ ☆

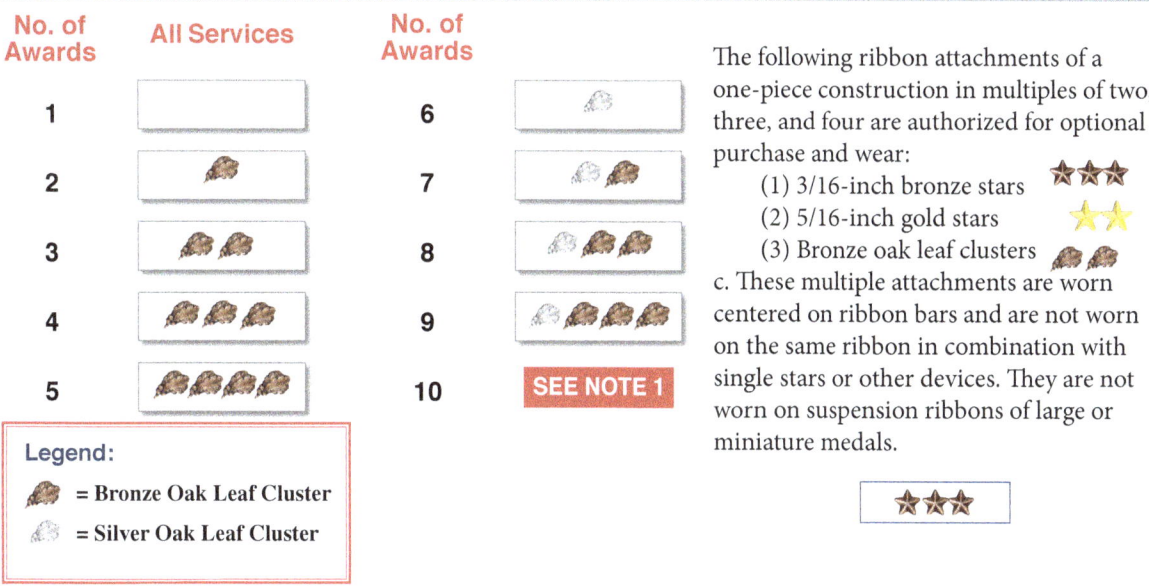

Placement of Oak Leaf Cluster Devices on the Ribbon

No. of Awards	All Services	No. of Awards	
1		6	(silver)
2	(bronze)	7	(silver, bronze)
3	(2 bronze)	8	(silver, 2 bronze)
4	(3 bronze)	9	(silver, 3 bronze)
5	(4 bronze)	10	SEE NOTE 1

Legend:
- 🍂 = Bronze Oak Leaf Cluster
- 🍂 = Silver Oak Leaf Cluster

The following ribbon attachments of a one-piece construction in multiples of two, three, and four are authorized for optional purchase and wear:
(1) 3/16-inch bronze stars ★★★
(2) 5/16-inch gold stars ★★
(3) Bronze oak leaf clusters 🍂🍂

c. These multiple attachments are worn centered on ribbon bars and are not worn on the same ribbon in combination with single stars or other devices. They are not worn on suspension ribbons of large or miniature medals.

Device Usage on the Navy Air Medal

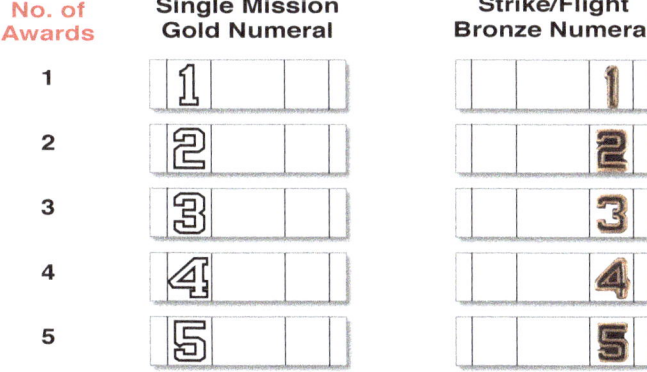

Navy (Individual Awards)

| 1 V 1 | 2 V 2 |

Since April 5, 1974, the Combat "V" may be authorized for awards for heroism or meritorious action in conflict with an armed enemy.

Ribbon devices (1989–2006)

Between November 22, 1989, and September 27, 2006, 3/16 inch bronze stars, 5/16 inch gold stars, and 5/16 inch silver stars denoted the number of "Individual" Air Medals. A bronze star denoted a first award. Gold stars were used for the second through the fifth awards with Silver stars used for five gold stars. For "Individual" Air Medals, the Combat "V" could be authorized.

Bronze Strike/Flight numerals denoted the number of Strike/Flight awards authorized for operations in hostile or disputed territory and count the total number of Strikes (operations that faced enemy opposition) and Flights (operations that did not encounter enemy opposition) added together.

Air Medal Device Arrangements. As of September 27, 2006, gold Numeral devices are used to denote the number of "Individual" Air Medals.

Bronze Strike/Flight numerals denote the total number of Strike/Flight awards. Strikes are combat sorties that encounter enemy opposition. Flights are combat sorties that do not encounter enemy opposition.

C Combat & R Remote Device Placement on the Ribbon

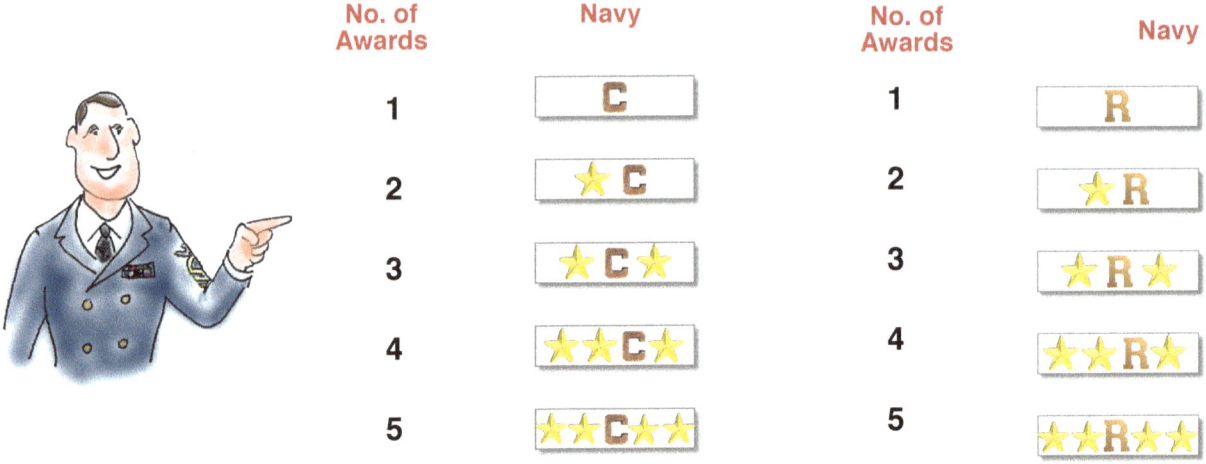

No. of Awards	Navy	No. of Awards	Navy
1	C	1	R
2	★C	2	★R
3	★C★	3	★R★
4	★★C★	4	★★R★
5	★★C★★	5	★★R★★

When both C and R device are awarded the C goes before the R and the V before both.

Right Breast Displays on U.S. Navy Full Dress Uniforms

The three Naval Services prescribe the wear of "ribbon only" awards on the right breast of the full dress uniform when large medals are worn. The Navy and Coast Guard align their ribbons inboard to outboard while the Marines align theirs outboard to inboard.

	Navy Presidential Unit Citation	Combat Action Ribbon	
Navy Meritorious Unit Commendation	Navy Unit Commendation	Joint Meritorious Unit Award
Fleet Marine Force Ribbon	Reserve Special Commendation Ribbon	Navy "E" Ribbon
Navy Reserve Sea Service Service Ribbon	Arctic Service Ribbon	Sea Service Deployment Ribbon
Navy Recruit Training Service Ribbon	Navy Recruiting Service Ribbon	Navy & Marine Corps Overseas Service Ribbon
Philippine Presidential Unit Citation	Navy Recruit Honor Graduate Ribbon	Navy Ceremonial Guard Ribbon
Vietnam Gallantry Cross Unit Citation	Vietnam Presidential Unit Citation	Korean Presidential Unit Ribbon
Philippine Liberation Ribbon	Philippine Defense Ribbon	Vietnam Civil Actions Unit Citation
Pistol Marksmanship Ribbon	Rifle Marksmanship Ribbon	Philippine Independence Ribbon

Officer, CPO and E1-E6 Ribbons with Medals

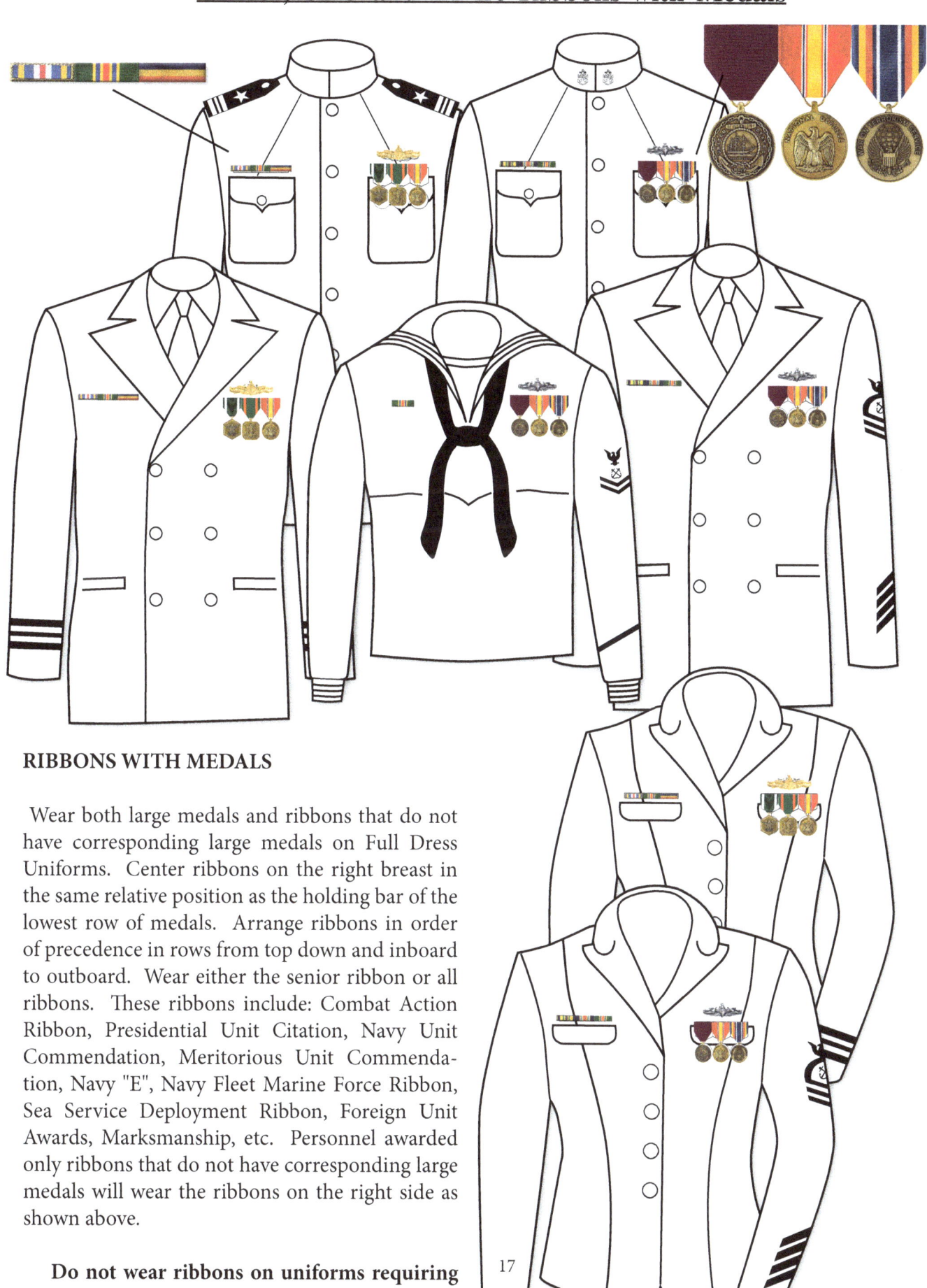

RIBBONS WITH MEDALS

Wear both large medals and ribbons that do not have corresponding large medals on Full Dress Uniforms. Center ribbons on the right breast in the same relative position as the holding bar of the lowest row of medals. Arrange ribbons in order of precedence in rows from top down and inboard to outboard. Wear either the senior ribbon or all ribbons. These ribbons include: Combat Action Ribbon, Presidential Unit Citation, Navy Unit Commendation, Meritorious Unit Commendation, Navy "E", Navy Fleet Marine Force Ribbon, Sea Service Deployment Ribbon, Foreign Unit Awards, Marksmanship, etc. Personnel awarded only ribbons that do not have corresponding large medals will wear the ribbons on the right side as shown above.

Do not wear ribbons on uniforms requiring miniature medals.

Male Officer and CPO Ribbon Wear

Ribbons are worn on the service coat or jumper of Service Dress Blue, Dress White, and on the shirt of Service Khaki. Wear up to three ribbons in a single row. When more than three ribbons are authorized, wear them in horizontal rows of three each. If ribbons are not in multiples of three, the top row contains the lesser number, and the center of this row sits over the center of the one below it. Wear ribbons without spaces between ribbons or rows of ribbons. Wear ribbons with the lower edge of the bottom row centered 1/4 inch above the left breast pocket and parallel to the deck. To prevent coat lapels from covering ribbons, ribbons may be aligned so the border to wearer's left is aligned with left side of pocket. Rows of ribbons where more than 50% of the ribbon is covered by the coat lapel may contain two ribbons each and be aligned with left border.

Placement on Ribbon Bar. Ribbons will be arranged on a bar(s) and attached to uniforms. Ribbons will not be impregnated with preservatives which change their appearance, or have any transparent covering.
Arrange ribbons in order of precedence in rows from top down, inboard to outboard. Wear either the three senior ribbons, or all ribbons if you have earned three or more.

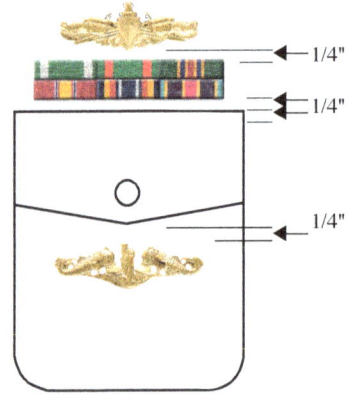

Qualification Insignia - When wearing ribbons, you may wear two qualification badges from any category for which you are qualified. When wearing two badges, put the most current or recently earned uppermost. With ribbons: the most recent badge is centered 1/4" above the ribbons. If a second badge is worn, it is centered 1/4" below the top of the left pocket.

Male Officer, CPO and E6-E1 Medal Wear

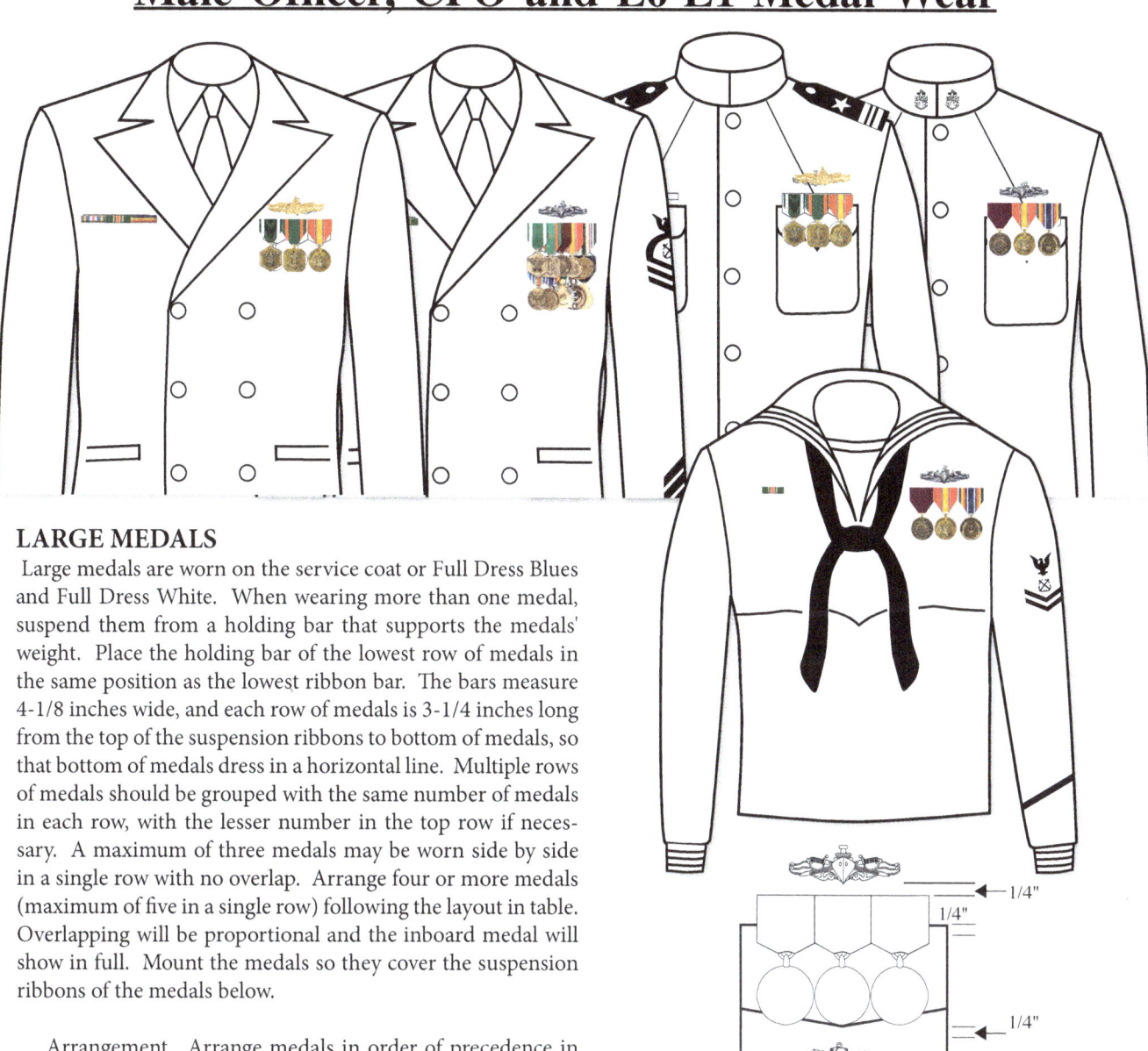

LARGE MEDALS

Large medals are worn on the service coat or Full Dress Blues and Full Dress White. When wearing more than one medal, suspend them from a holding bar that supports the medals' weight. Place the holding bar of the lowest row of medals in the same position as the lowest ribbon bar. The bars measure 4-1/8 inches wide, and each row of medals is 3-1/4 inches long from the top of the suspension ribbons to bottom of medals, so that bottom of medals dress in a horizontal line. Multiple rows of medals should be grouped with the same number of medals in each row, with the lesser number in the top row if necessary. A maximum of three medals may be worn side by side in a single row with no overlap. Arrange four or more medals (maximum of five in a single row) following the layout in table. Overlapping will be proportional and the inboard medal will show in full. Mount the medals so they cover the suspension ribbons of the medals below.

Arrangement. Arrange medals in order of precedence in rows from top down, inboard to outboard, within rows. Service members possessing more than five medals may either wear the five senior medals or all of them.

Wearing of Large and Miniature Medals by Navy Male Personnel

Total Number of Medals	Number of Rows	Number of Medals First Row	Number of Medals 2d Row	Number of Medals 3rd Row
1-5	1 row only	1-5	-	-
6	2	3	3	-
7	2	3	4	-
8	2	4	4	-
9	2	4	5	-
10	2	5	5	-
11	3	3	4	4
12	3	4	4	4
13	3	3	5	5
14	3	4	5	5

Male Officer, CPO and E6-E1 Miniature Medal Wear

MINIATURE MEDALS

Wear miniature medals with all formal dress uniforms and dinner dress uniforms. Each row of miniatures is 2-1/4 inches long, from top of the suspension ribbons to bottom of medals, so the bottom of medals dress in a horizontal line.

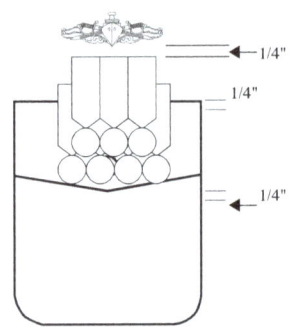

Position medals so they cover the suspension ribbons of the medals in the rows below. Male officers and CPOs, and E6 and below: on formal and dinner dress jackets, place the holding bar of the lowest row of miniature medals 3 inches below the notch, centered on the lapel, parallel to the deck. On blue and white service coats, center the holding bar 1/4 inch above the left breast pocket parallel to the deck. Female officers and CPOs, and E6 and below: on formal dress or dinner dress jackets, place the holding bar in the same relative position as on the men's dinner dress jackets, down 1/3 the distance between the shoulder seam and coat hem. On blue and white coats, center the holding bar 1/4 inch above the left pocket flap parallel to the deck. E6 and Below: on jumper uniforms, men and women place the holding bar of the lowest row of miniature medals 1/4 inch above the pocket parallel to the deck.

Arrangement. Wear up to five miniature medals in a row with no overlap. Arrange six or more miniature medals following the layout in the table.

a. Arrange medals in order of precedence in rows from top down, inboard to outboard, within rows. Service members possessing five or more medals may either wear the five senior medals or all of them. On the dinner dress jacket, center up to three miniature medals on the lapel. Position four or more miniatures starting at the inner edge of the lapel extending beyond the lapel on to the body of the jacket.

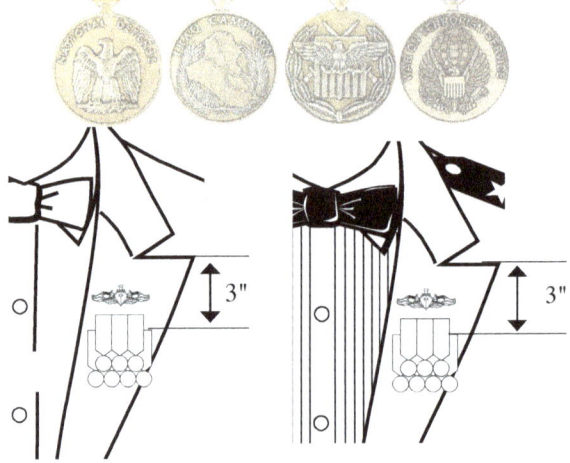

Female Officer and CPO Ribbon Wear

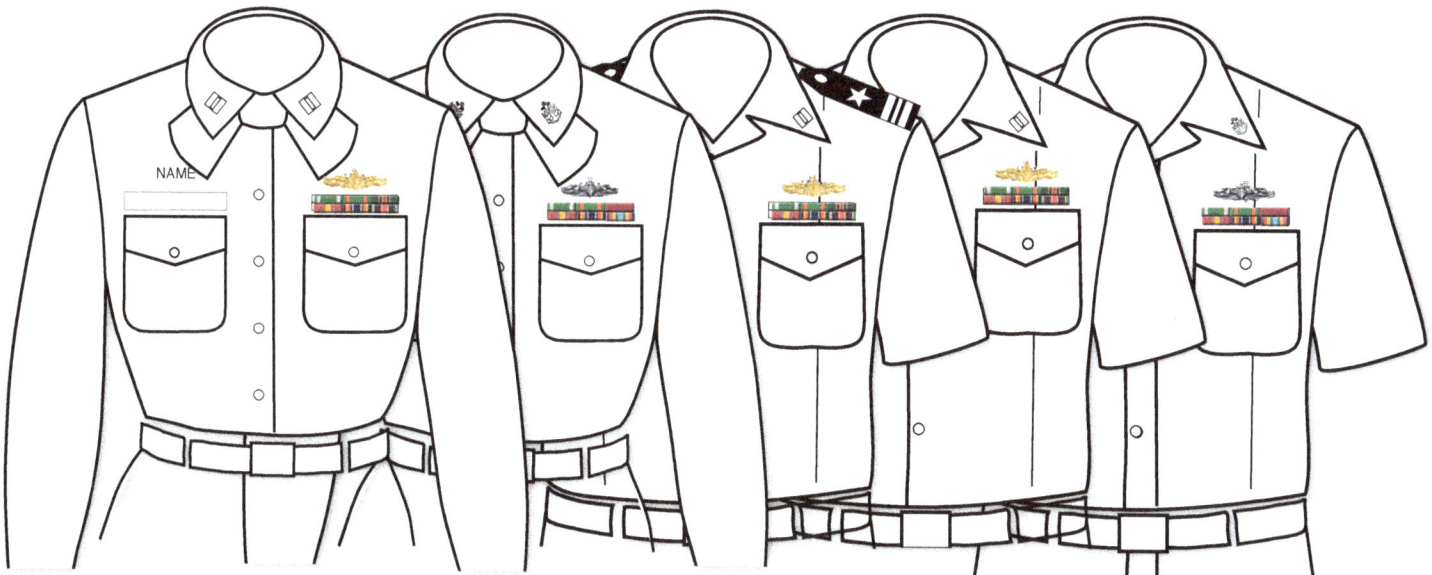

Ribbons are worn on the service coat or jumper of Service Dress Blue, Dress White, and on the shirt of Service Khaki. Wear up to three ribbons in a single row. When more than three ribbons are authorized, wear them in horizontal rows of three each. If ribbons are not in multiples of three, the top row contains the lesser number, and the center of this row sits over the center of the one below it. Wear ribbons without spaces between ribbons or rows of ribbons. Wear ribbons with the lower edge of the bottom row centered 1/4 inch above the left breast pocket and parallel to the deck. To prevent coat lapels from covering ribbons, ribbons may be aligned so the border to wearer's left is aligned with left side of pocket.

Rows of ribbons where more than 50% of the ribbon is covered by the coat lapel may contain two ribbons each and be aligned with left border.

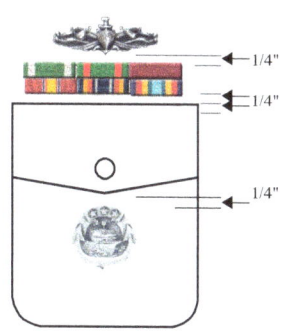

Qualification Insignia - When wearing ribbons, you may wear two qualification badges from any category for which you are qualified. When wearing two badges, put the most current or recently earned uppermost. With ribbons: the most recent badge is centered 1/4" above the ribbons. If a second badge is worn, it is centered 1/4" below the top of the left pocket.

Officer, CPO and E6-E1 Female Full Size Medal Wear

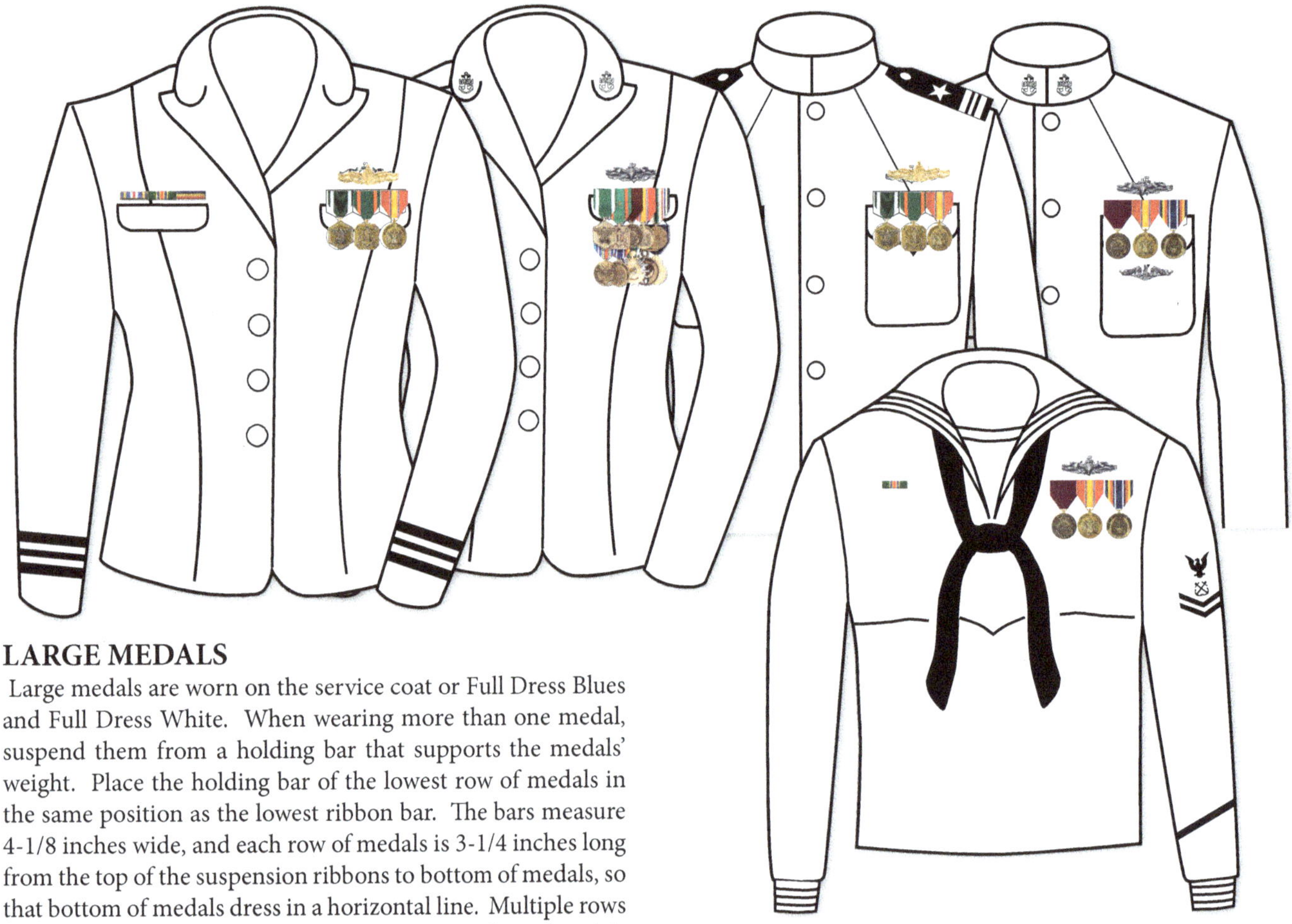

LARGE MEDALS

Large medals are worn on the service coat or Full Dress Blues and Full Dress White. When wearing more than one medal, suspend them from a holding bar that supports the medals' weight. Place the holding bar of the lowest row of medals in the same position as the lowest ribbon bar. The bars measure 4-1/8 inches wide, and each row of medals is 3-1/4 inches long from the top of the suspension ribbons to bottom of medals, so that bottom of medals dress in a horizontal line. Multiple rows of medals should be grouped with the same number of medals in each row, with the lesser number in the top row if necessary. A maximum of three medals may be worn side by side in a single row with no overlap. Arrange four or more medals (maximum of five in a single row) following the layout in table. Overlapping will be proportional and the inboard medal will show in full. Mount the medals so they cover the suspension ribbons of the medals below.

Arrangement. Arrange medals in order of precedence in rows from top down, inboard to outboard, within rows. Service members possessing more than five medals may either wear the five senior medals or all of them.

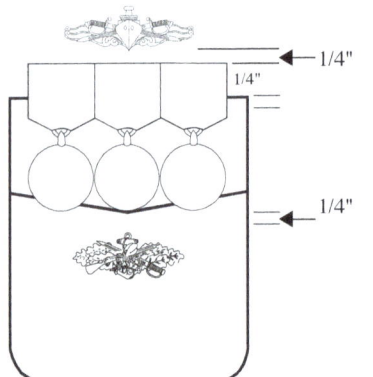

Wearing of Large and Miniature Medals by Navy Female Personnel

Total Number of Medals	Number of Rows	Number of Medals First Row	Number of Medals 2d Row	Number of Medals 3rd Row
1-5	1 row only	1-5	-	-
6	2	3	3	-
7	2	3	4	-
8	2	4	4	-
9	2	4	5	-
10	2	5	5	-
11	3	3	4	4
12	3	4	4	4

Officer, CPO and E6-E1 Female Miniature Size Medal Wear

MINIATURE MEDALS

Wear miniature medals with all formal dress uniforms and dinner dress uniforms. Each row of miniatures is 2-1/4 inches long, from top of the suspension ribbons to bottom of medals, so the bottom of medals dress in a horizontal line.

Position medals so they cover the suspension ribbons of the medals in the rows below.

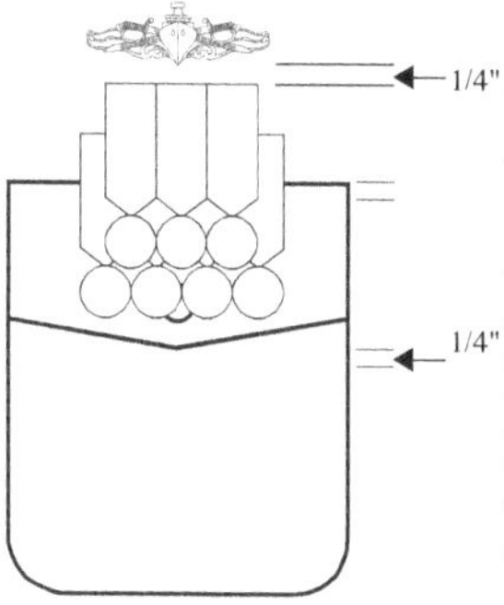

Female officers and CPOs, and E6 and below: on formal dress or dinner dress jackets, place the holding bar in the same relative position as on the men's dinner dress jackets, down 1/3 the distance between the shoulder seam and coat hem.

On blue and white coats, center the holding bar 1/4 inch above the left pocket flap parallel to the deck. E6 and Below: on jumper uniforms, men and women place the holding bar of the lowest row of miniature medals 1/4 inch above the pocket parallel to the deck.

. Arrangement. Wear up to five miniature medals in a row with no overlap. Arrange six or more miniature medals following the layout in the table to the left.

a. Arrange medals in order of precedence in rows from top down, inboard to outboard, within rows. Service members possessing five or more medals may either wear the five senior medals or all of them. On the dinner dress jacket, center up to three miniature medals on the lapel. Position four or more miniatures starting at the inner edge of the lapel extending beyond the lapel on to the body of the jacket.

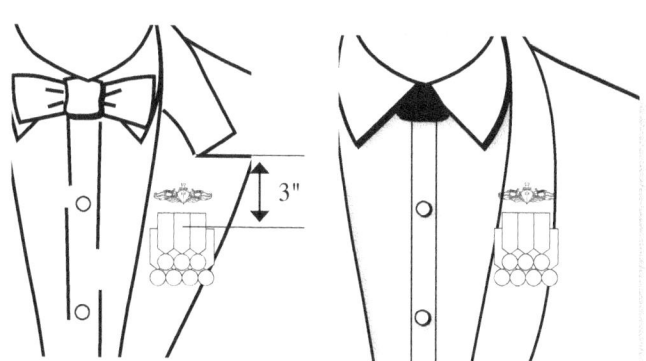

Place the holding bar in the same relative position as on the men's dinner dress jackets, down 1/3 the distance between the shoulder seam and coat hem.

E1-E6 Male & Female Dress Blues and Whites

Ribbons are worn on the jumper of Service Dress Blue and Dress White. Wear up to three ribbons in a single row. When more than three ribbons are authorized, wear them in horizontal rows of three each. If ribbons are not in multiples of three, the top row contains the lesser number, and the center of this row sits over the center of the one below it. Wear ribbons without spaces between ribbons or rows of ribbons. Wear ribbons with the lower edge of the bottom row centered 1/4 inch above the left breast pocket and parallel to the deck.

Large Medals are worn on Full Dress Blues and Full Dress White. When wearing more than one medal, suspend them from a holding bar that supports the medals' weight. Place the holding bar of the lowest row of medals in the same position as the lowest ribbon bar. The bars measure 4-1/8 inches wide, and each row of medals is 3-1/4 inches long from the top of the suspension ribbons to bottom of medals, so that bottom of medals dress in a horizontal line. Multiple rows of medals should be grouped with the same number of medals in each row, with the lesser number in the top row if necessary. A maximum of three medals may be worn side by side in a single row with no overlap. Arrange four or more medals (maximum of five in a single row) following the layout in table. Overlapping will be proportional and the inboard medal will show in full. Mount the medals so they cover the suspension ribbons of the medals below. Arrange medals in order of precedence in rows from top down, inboard to outboard, within rows. Service members possessing more than five medals may either wear the five senior medals or all of them.

Miniature medals for E6 and Below: on jumper uniforms, men and women place the holding bar of the lowest row of miniature medals 1/4 inch above the pocket parallel to the deck. Arrange miniatures the same as for full size medals i.e. in order of precedence in rows from top down, inboard to outboard, within rows.